SAVED FOR POSTERITY

BUS AND COACH PRESERVATION

KEITH A. JENKINSON

AMBERLEY

First published 2018

Amberley Publishing
The Hill, Stroud
Gloucestershire, GL5 4EP

www.amberley-books.com

Copyright © Keith A. Jenkinson, 2018

The right of Keith A. Jenkinson to be identified
as the Author of this work has been asserted
in accordance with the Copyright, Designs and
Patents Act 1988.

ISBN 978 1 4456 7496 4 (print)
ISBN 978 1 4456 7497 1 (ebook)

British Library Cataloguing in Publication Data.
A catalogue record for this book is available from
the British Library.

Origination by Amberley Publishing.
Printed in the UK.

Introduction

Although private bus preservation did not start until 1956, it was back in the 1920s that the collecting of historic passenger carrying vehicles first began when London General Omnibus Company took the decision to preserve an example of several of its main types of buses, all of which have fortunately survived today as part of the London Transport Museum. In addition, a tiny handful of other bus and coach operators have also preserved examples of their early fleet, while in more recent times others such as Stagecoach have seen the value of nostalgia and have retained a number of their buses after their working lives came to an end.

Looking specifically at private preservation, this began in 1956 when a group in London headed by Prince Marshall purchased a former London Transport 1929 AEC Regal single-deck bus after making an aborted attempt to acquire a similarly aged London double-decker. Difficulties quickly began to surface, however, with under-cover accommodation proving to be too expensive at that time, forcing outdoor storage to have to suffice, which led to the bus soon starting to suffer from the elements. Nevertheless, it had been saved from the scrapman's torch, and it happily still survives today, having been completely rebuilt in the meantime. Very soon after this, Colin Shears at Winkleigh, Devon, purchased a former Exeter Corporation 1938 Leyland TS8, and thus private bus preservation can be said to have been born. To cater for this new interest, and with the hope of encouraging others to follow suit, a national club was then formed under the title Vintage Passenger Vehicle Society, which was in 1963 subsumed into the Historic Commercial Vehicle Club (later Society).

Over the next few years several more buses of a past age were bought privately for preservation, and by 1962 their total had risen to sixty-one, with all examples having been built prior to the outbreak of the Second World War. Due largely to a lack of funds, however, restoration in those far off days was undertaken with little in the form of tools and equipment, but at least these early vehicles had survived. Most would ultimately be returned to their original glory – although due to a lack of knowledge and skills, a tiny handful fell by the wayside and were eventually scrapped. As the years progressed, the standards of restoration improved considerably, and while today this often continues to be undertaken by individual or groups of owners, a number have, for various reasons, instead chosen to have their buses professionally restored or painted to enable them to be presented in 'as new' condition.

Those buses that have been saved for posterity each have a history of their own, and while some have been purchased straight out of revenue-earning service and have thus been in good condition, others have been found in scrapyards, hidden on farms or caravan sites, and have consequently needed an enormous amount of work to bring them back to mobility and originality.

As the hobby continued to gain momentum, numerous more buses were purchased for preservation, and by 2017 their number had risen to more than 7,000. Together, they represent a wide variety of makes and models spanning from the early 1900s through to the new millennium. Many of these can be seen each year at historic vehicle events across the UK, while others can be viewed in various bus museums set up by enthusiasts, and all bring back memories of a past age in some form or other.

While it is not possible to illustrate every bus that has survived into preservation, I have tried within these pages to show a selection of those that have endured the passage of time. Although a number of the photographs are from my own camera, without the help of others there would have been several gaps. To all these people who have allowed me to use their work, I extend my sincere thanks, and am delighted to credit them in the captions. I offer my sincere apologies to those whose photographs unfortunately remain unknown to me (credited as 'Author's collection'), but I hope that they will gain pleasure in seeing their work in print.

How it all began. Believed to be the first bus to be privately preserved, former London General 1929 vintage LGOC-bodied AEC Regal T31 (UU 6646) is seen here after being totally restored and rebuilt to its original rear-entrance specification. (D. W. Rhodes)

Representing the early days of the motor bus is the superbly restored, solid rubber-tyred, Leyland X-type double-decker LN 7270, which began life in June 1908 with the London Central Omnibus Company. (D. W. Rhodes)

Among the oldest buses to be preserved is EC 634, a twelve-seat Commer MC that was purchased new by the Earl of Lonsdale in 1909. It is seen here approaching Brighton on the HCVS Run from London in May 2002. (F. W. York)

New to London General Omnibus Co. in 1912, immaculately restored AEC B-type B1609 (LF 8375) leaves Crystal Palace, London, at the start of the annual HCVS Run to Brighton in May 2017. (D. W. Rhodes)

A unique vehicle, 1913 All American C 56 was fitted with its replica twenty-seat charabanc body in 1973. (Author's collection)

New to the London & North Western Railway in July 1914, superbly restored Leyland S4 charabanc CC 1087 is now part of the London Transport Museum collection. (Nigel Eadon-Clarke)

Fitted with a replica body in 1968, Crossley 20/25 DB 2243, the chassis of which was new in 1915, enters Harrogate on an HCVS Trans-Pennine Run, followed by ex-SHMD 1956 vintage NCME-bodied Daimler CVD6 76 (VTU 76) and 1951 Duple-bodied Albion FT39N LAO 630. (Author's collection)

All now owned by the London Transport Museum are: ex-London General Brush-bodied AEC K-type K424 (XC 8059), which was new in November 1920; ex-London General LGOC-bodied AEC S-type S433 (XL 8940) of October 1922; former Chocolate Express Dodson-bodied Leyland LB5 XU 7498, which was new in August 1924; and ex-London General LGOC-bodied AEC NS-type NS1995 (YR 3844), which began life in February 1927. (David Hudson collection)

Typifying the long-wheelbase Ford Model TT is DX 3426, which began life in 1922, owned by the Halstead Omnibus Company. It is pictured here in May 2002. (F. W. York)

Owned by the National Motor Museum at Beaulieu, and seen en route to Brighton in May 2002, is CJ 5052, a 1922 fourteen-seat Maxwell 25 cwt charabanc. (F. W. York)

Now part of the Barton Cherished Vehicle Collection at Beeston, Nottingham, is 1923 vintage Daimler CJS W 963, which was originally registered NW 7341 and gained its replica charabanc body in 1953. (Author's collection)

Purchased new in April 1925 by London independent London Public, forty-eight-seat Dodson-bodied Dennis 3-ton XX 9591 passed to London General Omnibus Co. (in whose livery it is preserved) in 1933 and was given fleet number D142. Fitted with pneumatic tyres, it is now owned by the London Bus Preservation Trust. (Nigel Eadon-Clarke)

Another ex-London bus is the privately owned, superbly restored former Thomas Tilling XW 9892 – a Tilling-Stevens TS7 petrol electric single-decker that was new in 1925. It is pictured here in 2017 taking part in the HCVS London to Brighton Run. (D. W. Rhodes)

Seen here on the 2017 HCVS London to Brighton Run is Tilling-Stevens Express B9A MO 9324, which was purchased new by Thames Valley Omnibus Co. in June 1927 and was given its new replica body in 1998. (D. W. Rhodes)

Also new in June 1927, albeit to Southdown, is this superbly restored nineteen-seat Short Bros-bodied Dennis 30 cwt (UF 1517), which is a resident at the Southdown Omnibus Trust's museum at Amberley. (F. W. York)

Returned to the UK in 1958 after spending twenty-six years in service in Jersey, Leyland Lion PLSC3 KW 1961, which was new to Blythe & Berwick, Bradford, in July 1927, is seen in 2017 after being completely restored to its original condition and livery.

New to the Great Western Railway in March 1927, Vickers-bodied Guy FBB YF 714 is seen here alongside former London General AEC B-type B2737 (LH 8186) in the livery worn by these buses when used by the Army in Europe during the First World War. (David Hudson collection)

Although its Short Bros body was new in December 1928, the Leyland N-type chassis of ex-Southdown CD 5125 dates from November 1920. Now fully restored, the bus is part of the Stagecoach historic vehicle collection. (T. S. Blackman)

Showing the condition of some of the buses that have been acquired for preservation is former Colne Corporation 1928 Leyland Lion PLSC3 TE 5110, which had been used as a summer caravan near Blackpool. Here it is seen being collected in March 1973 after being purchased by the author, who later sold it to the Transport Museum Society of Ireland for restoration.

In pristine condition after a long-term, thorough restoration is former Ashton Corporation English Electric-bodied tri-axle Karrier WL6 TE 5780, which was new in November 1928. (David Hudson)

Preserved on the Isle of Man, where it spent all its operating life, is Hall Lewis-bodied Thornycroft BC 13 (MN 5454), which was new in 1928 and has now been superbly restored. (Author's collection)

New to Sunderland Corporation in May 1929, all-Leyland Lion LT1 2 (BR 7132) spent a large part of its life with Jersey Motor Transport before being repatriated to England for preservation in 1959. (T. S. Blackman)

Seen attending a rally at Batley, West Yorkshire, in June 1969 are: VO 6806, a 1931 Craven-bodied AEC Regal; J 1199, a 1931 all-Leyland TD1 that spent all its working life in Jersey; and DM 6228, a former Brookes Bros, Rhyl, Burlingham charabanc-bodied Leyland Lioness LTB1 from 1929.

Now part of the FirstGroup Heritage Trust at Alford, Walker-bodied Albion PMA28 RG 1173, which was new to Aberdeen Corporation in April 1930, is seen here at Brighton – a long way from home – on the HCVS Run from London in May 2002. (F. W. York)

Restored in the livery of its original owner, Thomas Tilling, who purchased it in November 1930, ST922 (GJ 2098) passed to London Transport in 1933 and was sold in 1955 after serving as a mobile canteen since 1947. Found in a scrapyard in 1966, it was then totally restored and used on a heritage bus service in the capital for a few years before being retired, ultimately passing to the London Bus Preservation Group. (D. W. Rhodes)

New to Llandudno UDC in April 1930, who used it on tours around the Great Orme, is CC 9424, a Roberts toastrack-bodied Dennis GL. (Dennis Society)

Seen at Brighton at the end of the HCVC Run from London is Weymann-bodied Gilford 168OT GW 713, which had been restored in the livery it originally carried when new in 1931. (Author's collection)

Typifying early Bedford coaches is HB 4060, a 1931 Davies-bodied WTB model which started life in South Wales with Williams of Blaina. (F. W. York)

Immaculately restored as a reminder of London Transport's well-loved three-axle AEC Renowns, which were affectionately known as 'Scooters', LT1076 (GO 5198) began life with London General Omnibus Co. in May 1931 and is now owned by the London Transport Museum. (D. W. Rhodes)

With its Leyland TD1 chassis dating from 1928 and its Eastern Counties Coach Works lowbridge body from 1932, JUB 29 was purchased by the author for preservation in 1963 and is seen here in 2017 restored to its 1932 Keighley West Yorkshire condition and livery.

New in March 1932 to Alfreton independent operator Fox with this 1929 Reeve & Kenning body is superbly restored fourteen-seat Commer Centaur RB 4757. (Author's collection)

Originally used by Entwistle, Morecambe, on day excursions, and now back in the care of its manufacturer, Duple-bodied Dennis Dart TJ 836 was first licenced in March 1933.

New to Western National in June 1933, Bristol H5G 137 (FJ 8967) was given its Bristol body in October 1942, and after serving with a showman from 1957, was purchased for preservation twelve years later. It is seen here after being superbly restored, complete with wartime white wing tips and guard rail. (Ian Winchester)

New to Rhondda Tramways in 1933, AEC Regent TG 6211 was given its prototype Welsh Metal Industries body in 1947, and is seen here in 2017 shortly after being rescued for preservation. (David Hudson collection)

Purchased for preservation in the late 1950s, ex-Lytham St Annes all-Leyland LT5A TJ 6760, seen here at Brighton on the 1964 HCVC Run from London, began life as a demonstrator in October 1934. Towards the end of the 1960s it was exported to Canada by its preservationist owner, but after being abandoned it was returned to the UK in a derelict condition in December 1998. It has since been fully restored to its original glory.

Safely preserved by the London Transport Museum is this former London AEC Regent STL469 (AYV 651), which was new in July 1934 and is seen here taking part in the 2017 HCVS London to Brighton Run. (D. W. Rhodes)

Fitted with a Harrington body dating from 1947, and seen here on an HCVS Trans-Pennine Run, the chassis of former Charlie's Cars Albion Valiant PV70 LJ 9501 was new in March 1934.

Restored as a convertible open topper is former Portsmouth Corporation English Electric-bodied Leyland TD4 5 (RV 6358), which began life in July 1935. (T. S. Blackman)

The AEC Q was unusual in having its engine mounted at the side, behind its front axle. Representing this model are Birmingham Railway Carriage & Wagon Co.-bodied Q55 (BXD 576), which is preserved by the London Transport Museum, and Q86 (CGJ 18), which is now owned by the London Bus Preservation Trust. Although both were new in country area green livery in 1935, and remained in service until 1953, Q86 is seen here representing the red livery some carried while operated in the central area from 1948. (Nigel Eadon-Clarke)

New to West Riding Automobile Company in 1936, twenty-four-seat Roe-bodied Leyland Cub KPZ2 HL 7538 spent much of its life with Pritchard, Newburgh, Anglesey, in whose livery it is preserved – as seen here in 2015.

This 1936 Underwood-bodied Morris Commercial C-type spent all its working life in Jersey, but is seen here awaiting restoration by its current owner, Aire Valley Preservation Group, Bradford. (AVPG)

Looking immaculate after being professionally restored is ex-Ribble, coach-liveried, Brush-bodied Leyland Cheetah LZ2 1568 (RN 7824), which was new in June 1936. (Cobus)

Although given its new rear-entrance ECW body in 1949, ex-United Counties 1937 Bristol JO5G 450 (VV 5696) unusually retained its high 'shield type' Bristol radiator. (T. S. Blackman)

New to Stockport Corporation in January 1937, English Electric centre entrance-bodied Leyland TS7 JA 7591 is seen here en route to Brighton on the HCVC Run from London in May 1968.

When new in July 1937, East Kent Dennis Lancet II JG 8720 was fitted with a Dennis body, but in 1949 it was given the new Park Royal body with which it is seen here. (T. S. Blackman)

Also rebodied was former Maidstone & District 1937 Leyland TS7 CO558 (DKT 16), which was given its new Harrington body in 1950, featuring a band box set into its roof. (T. S. Blackman)

Entering service with London Transport as Green Line coach T499 in July 1938, and now preserved by Ensignbus, Purfleet, LPTB-bodied AEC Regal ELP 223 is seen here in 2013 wearing the American Red Cross livery it carried while on loan to the USAAF during the Second World War. It has since been repainted in its original Green Line colours. (Nigel Eadon-Clarke)

Among the first buses to be privately preserved was former Exeter Corporation 66 (EFJ 666), a Leyland TS8 with a Craven body that features a cut-away rear platform entrance. New in December 1938, it was acquired by Devon enthusiast Colin Shears in 1956. (Author's collection)

Both new to London Transport in 1939 with bodies built at its Chiswick works, AEC Regent RT8 (FXT 183) was later sold to the USA and was repatriated in April 2006, while rear-engined Leyland Cub CR16 (FXT 122) found a new home in Cyprus, returning to the UK in 1979. Both buses are seen here after being totally restored as reminders of a past age. (D. W. Rhodes)

BMMO (Midland Red) built its own chassis for more than four decades under the SOS title (Shire's Own Specification, derived from its designer L. G. Wyndham Shire, who was BMMO's chief engineer). Illustrated here is beautifully preserved SON GHA 337, which, fitted with a thirty-eight-seat Brush body, was new in 1940. (T. S. Blackman)

This view at Keighley Bus Museum of two former Leeds City Transport AEC Regents allows the comparison of the Roe body styles of 1934 vintage 139 (ANW 682) and 1940 106 (HUM 401). (Author's collection)

Despite being colloquially known as 'pre-war RTs', these buses were not placed in service until 1940 (except for RT1). Here, RT44 (FXT 219) is seen in Brighton in May 1965, a few months after being bought for preservation.

Built after the outbreak of the Second World War, albeit to pre-war design, is ex-United ECW-bodied Bristol L5G BG147 (FHN 833), which first entered service in January 1941 and has been superbly restored by its current owners, the Lincolnshire Vintage Vehicle Society. (Author's collection)

The only new single-deck model build during the Second World War was the Bedford OWB (based on the pre-war OB chassis), fitted with standard design utility bodywork. Seen here fitted with a replica body built in 1985, and painted in Northern Ireland Road Transport livery, is V957 (GZ 783), which is preserved by Translink (Ulsterbus). (Paul Savage)

Starting life in January 1945 as a conventional closed top Southdown double-decker, NCME-bodied Guy Arab II GUF 191 was converted to open top for coastal tourist services before being sold to a museum in Denmark. Repatriated to the UK in 2002 for restoration, it is seen here before the work commenced. (F. W. York)

Typifying buses built during the Second World War is former Northampton Corporation Duple-bodied Daimler CWD6 129 (VV 8934), which was new in June 1945. It is seen here passing preserved ex-Lincolnshire Road Car Co. Bristol LD6B Lodekka 2318 (LFW 326). (Author's collection)

New in July 1945, ex-Western National Bristol K6A 353 (FTT 704) had its original Strachan body replaced with a new ECW lowbridge one in 1955; at the same time, it was also given a PV2 radiator. It has been in private preservation since February 1972. (F. W. York)

Despite being built to wartime specification, ex-London Transport Park Royal-bodied Guy Arab II G351 (HGC130) was new in January 1946, and is seen here alongside Dodson-bodied Dennis 3-ton D142 (XX 9591), which began life with independent London Public in April 1925. (Nigel Eadon-Clarke)

Built as a conventional single-decker in November 1946, Maidstone & District Beadle-bodied AEC Regal I HKL 819 was, along with two of its sisters, converted to open-top format in 1957, as illustrated here in preservation. (T. S. Blackman)

New in February 1946 to London Transport's country area are: Weymann-bodied AEC Regent II STL2692 (HGC 225), which later served with Grimsby Corporation and is seen here on the 1968 HCVC London to Brighton Run prior to being restored to its original owner's livery; ex-City of Oxford Willowbrook-bodied AEC Regal III 703 (OJD 703), which was new in 1949; and former London Transport Weymann-bodied AEC RT191 (HLW 178), which entered service in October 1947.

Fitted with a Brislington body in June 1947, AHU 803 is actually a Bristol JO5G. It started life in April 1934 with Bristol Tramways and was purchased for preservation in 1978. (Author's collection)

Meticulously restored to as new condition, and sporting a familiar 'Shop at Binns' advert on its front upper deck panels, is former Sunderland Corporation all-Crossley DD42/3 13 (GR 9007), which was new in 1947. (T. S. Blackman)

Park Royal deck-and-a-half-bodied Commer Commandos were used by airlines such as BEA and BOAC, as well as by the armed forces shortly after the Second World War. Superbly restored XAT 368 was new to the Royal Air Force in April 1947 and is now preserved at the Yorkshire Air Museum at Elvington. (Author's collection)

Fitted with a Strachan body and delivered new to Crosville in November 1948, AEC Regal III TA5 (JFM 575) has been superbly restored to as new condition. (Ian Winchester)

Former Bristol Tramways ECW highbridge-bodied Leyland PD1A C4044 (LAE 13), which was new in March 1948, is seen here in June 1977 alongside ex-Barton Duple lowbridge-bodied Leyland PD1 467 (JNN 384), which dates from December 1947. (F. W. York)

After spending the whole of its working life with Jersey Motor Transport, with whom it was numbered 71 and registered J11 429, Wadham-bodied Morris Commercial CVF13/5 OSJ 512, which was new in 1948, is seen here after being purchased by an English preservationist. (T. S. Blackman)

New in November 1948, Midland Red 3301 (KHA 301) is a Duple-bodied BMMO C1 coach that has been immaculately restored to its original condition in attractive red and black livery.

Once preserved and beautifully restored, but later sadly scrapped, is ex-Southdown all-Leyland highbridge PD2/1 JCD 81, which was new in 1948. (Author's collection)

After being displayed on the Maudslay stand at the 1948 Commercial Motor Show, Duple-bodied AEC Regal III HHP 755, which was surprisingly badged as a Maudslay, started life with Devon coach operator Greenslade's Tours, and has now been restored to as new condition. (Author's collection)

New to Accrington Corporation in February 1949, Guy Arab III KTC 615 carries a body built by Guy on Park Royal frames.

Typifying the standard ECW post-war single-deck bus body is former Bristol Omnibus Co. Bristol L6B 2388 (LHT 911), which was new in September 1948 and is seen here on the Isle of Man at a preserved vehicle rally in June 1984. Alongside is ex-Rawtenstall Corporation 1958 vintage East Lancs-bodied Leyland Tiger Cub 58 (466 FTJ) and former Isle of Man Road Services Weymann-bodied Leyland Tiger Cub 20 (WMN 6), which began life in July 1957.

Preserved by Manchester coach operator Bullocks of Cheadle, Foden PVSC6 LMA 284 was new in April 1949. As seen here, it was given a new Lawton body in 1960. (F. W. York)

Proving that not all early pre-war Bristols were fitted with ECW bodywork, former Wilts &
Dorset 1949 vintage L6B 279 (EMW 284) was given Beadle coachwork, as illustrated here.
(F. W. York)

Built for London Transport with a Leyland body to the same design as that fitted to the RTs and
RTLs, preserved 8-foot-wide Leyland 6RT RTW467 (LLU 957) was new in October 1950 and is
seen here at Brighton on the HCVC Run from London in May 1967.

Although all-Crossley SD42/7 DBN 978 was new to Bolton Corporation in September 1949, it has been restored in Manchester Corporation streamlined livery with wartime white wing tips and guard rails, as seen here in 2015.

New to West Yorkshire Road Car Co. in December 1938, Bristol K5G KDG26 (CWX 671) was fitted with a new Roe lowbridge body and Bristol PV2 radiator in 1950. Saved by the author from the breaker's torch in 1963, it has since had two further owners and is seen here in 2017 after a recent repaint.

Typifying the Duple-bodied Bedford OB coach, of which a large number were built between 1939 and 1951, is ACC 629, which was new in March 1950. It is seen here after being restored by its current coach operator owner, Bibby's of Ingleton. (Author's collection)

All new to Belfast Corporation and fitted with Harkness bodywork are: 346 (MZ7 444), a Guy Arab III that was new in February 1951; 446 (OZ 6700), a Daimler CVG6 that was new in November 1953; and 286 (MZ7 384), a Guy Arab III that was new in February 1950. All three have been preserved. (Paul Savage)

Immaculately restored in the livery of its final operational owner, Leeds independent Samuel Ledgard, is 1950 vintage Burlingham-bodied Leyland PS1/1 KUP 949, which is seen here in October 2017.

London Transport's first standard post-war double-decker was the AEC Regent III RT, of which 4,825 were built. Representing the type, of which numerous are preserved, is Weymann-bodied RT1798 (KYY 653), which was new in June 1950. (T. S. Blackman)

Starting life with South Yorkshire in January 1950 as a Burlingham-bodied single-deck coach registered JWT 112, this Albion Valiant CX39N was given a new Roe lowbridge body in May 1958 and re-registered TWY 8. It is now preserved, as seen here. (Scott Poole)

Fitted with a lowbridge body built by its operator, Ulster Transport Authority, now-preserved Leyland PD2/1 D927 (MZ 7789) entered service in October 1950 and is seen here restored to its original condition. (Paul Savage)

Although Duple was best known for its coach bodies, it did also build a number of double-deck bus bodies, one of which is seen here on preserved Guy Arab III HWO 342, which began life with Red & White in South Wales in March 1950. (D. W. Rhodes)

New to East Kent Road Car Co. in July 1950, Dennis Falcon EFN 568, with a twenty-seat body built by its chassis manufacturer, is seen here restored to its original glory. (Nigel Eadon-Clarke)

More often thought of as a goods model, the Leyland Comet was also adapted for use as a passenger carrying vehicle, as illustrated by Duple-bodied MHY 765, which was new in April 1950 and is seen here on the 2017 HCVS Trans-Pennine Run.

Former Crosville standard ECW-bodied Bristol LL6B SLB175 (LFM 756), which was new in October 1950, is seen here in preservation in March 2016, having been fitted with West Yorkshire Road Car Co. destination blinds.

Park Royal-bodied Guy Arab III GTP 484 was new to Southampton Corporation in July 1951, and is seen here with former BEA Park Royal deck-and-a-half-bodied AEC Regal IV MLL 738, which began life in 1952. (D. W. Rhodes)

Fitted with a Duple bus body, beautifully restored Bedford OB BEP 882 began life with independent operator Mid Wales at Newtown in March 1951. (D. W. Rhodes)

Successor to the Bedford OB was the Bedford SB; it is represented here by preserved Duple-bodied PPH 698, which was new in June 1951. (D. W. Rhodes)

During the 1930s, Birmingham Corporation developed a standard design double-deck bus body, which continued in production for around twenty years. Seen here are pre and post-war examples, both of which carry Metro Cammell bodies. 2707 (JOJ 707) is a Daimler CVD6 that was new in September 1951, while alongside is 1107 (CVP 207), a Daimler COG5 that entered service in November 1937 but carries a body built in 1939. (T. S. Blackman)

Fitted with a Park Royal body completed in the Dundalk workshops of its owner, GNR, in 1951, 390 (IY7 384) – which is now preserved by the Transport Museum Society of Ireland – has a chassis that was also built by its owner, and is powered by a Gardner engine. (Author's collection)

Built in April 1951 as a 'one-off' vehicle for Maidstone & District, sixteen-seat Harrington-bodied Commer Avenger I coach LC1 (NKN 650) has fortunately been preserved for posterity. (T. S. Blackman)

Painted in Royal Blue livery, Southern National's 1952 ECW coach-bodied Bristol LS6G 1286 (MOD 973), with a luggage carrier on the rear of its roof, typifies the coaches that plied between the South West and London in the early years of underfloor-engined vehicles. (D. W. Rhodes)

Believed to be the only surviving Mann Egerton-bodied deck-and-a-half coach, Leyland Royal Tiger JVB 908 was new in June 1952 and is seen here in 2016, restored in the livery of its original owner. (George Townsend)

Using pre-war Leyland running units, ex-Maidstone & District integrally constructed Beadle CO252 (OKP 980), which was new in March 1952, is seen on a preserved vehicle running day in 2007. Alongside is former London Transport RT HLW 159, which has been painted in Bradford City Transport livery.

In the early 1950s, London Transport replaced most of its single-deck buses with Metro Cammell-bodied AEC Regal IVs – one of which, RF429 (MXX 406), new in February 1953, is seen preserved in central area red livery. (D. W. Rhodes)

Still to be restored is preserved ECW lowbridge-bodied Bristol KSW6B HDL 68, which began life with Thames Valley Traction Co. in May 1953, and is pictured here in March 2016.

As replacements for its pre-war Leyland Cubs, London Transport purchased eighty-four ECW-bodied Guy Specials based on the Guy Vixen chassis. Unbelievably, twenty-six of these buses have been preserved – one of which, GS64 (MXX 364), seen here, first entered service in December 1953 and is now part of the London Transport Museum collection. (T. S. Blackman)

Built as a Weymann-bodied single-decker in December 1949, PMT Leyland OPD2/1 L453 (NEH 453) was given its 1951 Northern Counties lowbridge body (which had been removed from another vehicle) in 1954. (T. S. Blackman)

Restored with its original style bonnet and grille, one of London Transport's four prototype Routemasters – Weymann-bodied Leyland-engined RML3 (SLT 58), which made its debut in June 1957 – has thankfully been preserved by the London Bus Preservation Trust. (Nigel Eadon-Clarke).

Uniquely preserved in the UK is former American Greyhound GMC PD4501, deck-and-a-half tri-axle Scenicruiser UAS 576, which was new in 1954 and imported into the UK in 2003. (T. S. Blackman)

Caught by the camera in June 1998 is preserved ex-Southdown Park Royal-bodied Leyland PD2/12 772 (OCD 772), which is fitted with rear platform doors and half-drop windows, and was new in May 1955. (F. W. York)

Fortunately preserved, and seen here undergoing restoration, is Metro
Cammell-bodied Leyland Lowloader LFDD XTC 684, which was built in November
1955 as a prototype for the Leyland Atlantean, which ultimately made its debut
during the following year. (K. S. E. Till)

With lowbridge Park Royal bodywork, former Maidstone & District AEC Regent
V DL39 (VKR 39), which was new in March 1956 and has rear platform doors,
is seen here at Feversham in 2016, immaculately restored to as new condition.
(Nigel Eadon-Clarke)

Fitted with forty-one-seat Yeates Europa bodywork, Bedford SBG NKY 161 began life with Fairways, Bradford, in May 1957. It is now preserved by coach operator Dons of Great Dunmow. (T. S. Blackman)

Showing the domed roof of its Roe body to allow passage through the historic Beverley Bar is preserved former East Yorkshire Motor Services 1957 AEC Regent V 652 (WAT 652), which was new in November 1957.

Despite sporting a new full-front Reading body that was fitted in 1958, the Guy Arab II chassis of preserved Provincial (Gosport & Fareham) 17 (EOR 875) dates from April 1945, and was originally fitted with Park Royal bodywork. (F. W. York)

With its Harrington body having been modified for one-man operation (OMO) is former Maidstone & District AEC Reliance CO390 (390 DKK), which was new to the company in October 1958. (T. S. Blackman)

Starting life as a demonstrator in March 1958, after which it was purchased by Merthyr Tydfil UDC, Weymann-bodied Leyland Tiger Cub PSUC1/1 964 DTJ is seen here after being acquired for preservation. (D. W. Rhodes)

Fourteen-seat, Plaxton-bodied Karrier minicoach PFR 727, which was new in January 1959, is seen here taking part in the 2017 HCVS Trans-Pennine Run.

Typifying the ECW-bodied Bristol MW in its various forms is preserved ex-West Yorkshire Road Car Co. dual-purpose-configured MW5G EUG71 (TWT 123), which was new in May 1959 and made several appearances in the ITV drama *Heartbeat*.

Preserved in the livery of its original owner, Aldershot & District, by whom it was purchased new in January 1960, is Weymann-bodied AEC Reliance 370 (XHO 370). (F. W. York)

New to Hills, Tredegar, in June 1960 was preserved Burlingham-bodied Leyland Leopard L1 XWO 911. (D. W. Rhodes)

Fitted with stylish forty-one-seat Harrington Crusader coachwork, Bedford SB3 326 CAA was purchased new by King Alfred, Winchester, in August 1961. (D. W. Rhodes)

When new in May 1950, Hants & Dorset 677 (KEL 405) was a twenty-eight-seat Portsmouth Aviation coach-bodied Bristol L6G. In 1961, its chassis was extended to become an LL6B, and it was fitted with a new ECW thirty-nine-seat, full-fronted bus body, as seen here in June 1998. (F. W. York)

Almost exclusively operated by West Riding Automobile Co., the troublesome Guy Wulfrunians only had short lives before being largely disposed of to the scrapman. Happily, however, two have survived into preservation – one of which was Roe-bodied UCX 275, which was new in September 1961 painted in County livery, and is seen here restored in West Riding colours. (Author's collection)

Purchased new by Edinburgh Corporation in December 1961, Leyland Leopard PSU3/2R 101 (YSG 101) is fitted with an unusual three-door Alexander body and is seen here a long way from home on the 2013 HCVS Trans-Pennine Run.

With the upper-deck windows of its Park Royal body tapered inwards to allow it to pass beneath the fifteenth-century Beverley Bar, AEC Bridgemaster 725 (9725 AT) started life with East Yorkshire Motor Services in June 1962, and is seen here in 2017 after a complete restoration.

New to West Yorkshire Road Car Co. in November 1962, ECW bus-bodied Bristol SUL4A SMA5 (811 BWR) has been restored to its original condition, and is pictured here in Otley during a preserved vehicle running day in October 2017.

Built on an AEC Regent V chassis, a model usually associated with double-deck vehicles, is preserved former South Wales Transport Roe-bodied 38 (282 DWN), which was purchased new in 1963 to operate a service in Llanelli that passed under an ultra-low bridge. (D. W. Rhodes)

One of a number of ECW forward-entrance-bodied Bristol Lodekkas to be saved for posterity, FLF6G 2019 (824 KDV) began life with Western National in May 1963 and is seen here taking part in an HCVS Trans-Pennine Run.

Former Portsmouth Corporation Metro Cammell-bodied Leyland Atlantean PDR1/1 236 (BBK 236B) started life in September 1964, and had been restored to its original livery when seen here at Southsea in June 1998. (F. W. York)

Representing Southdown's much loved full-fronted 'Queen Marys' is NCME-bodied Leyland PD3/4 972 (972 CUF), which entered service in June 1964 and is seen here immaculately restored to 'as new' condition. (T. S. Blackman)

Featuring all the attributes of the Bristol Lodekka, and built under licence by Dennis as its Loline model, former Aldershot & District AAA 503C is a forward-entrance, Weymann-bodied Mk III that was new in January 1965. (T. S. Blackman)

Preserved RML2272 (CUV 272C) shows the additional bay added into the body of London Transport's 30-foot-long Park Royal-bodied AEC Routemasters. (Nigel Eadon-Clarke)

Although built in July 1965 for King Alfred, Winchester, with a Plaxton Panorama body, the one now fitted (as seen here) to Bedford VAL14 CCG 704C was built in 1967 and was transferred in 2001 from a similar chassis coach owned by Leon, Finningley. (T. S. Blackman)

Displaying the classic lines of its ECW bus body is preserved Bristol MW6G U765 (DAX 610C), which was new to Red & White in May 1965. (D. W. Rhodes)

New to York-West Yorkshire in December 1966, and typifying the ECW-bodied Bristol Lodekka FS6B, is preserved YDX221 (NWU 265D), which has platform doors fitted to its rear entrance.

Starting life with Southampton Corporation in December 1967, Neepsend-bodied AEC Regent V 402 (KOW 910F) is now preserved. (F. W. York)

Roe-bodied Leyland Atlantean PDR1/1 163 (OBU 163F) was new to Oldham Corporation in December 1967 and was later absorbed into SELNEC (Greater Manchester PTE). It is seen here having been restored to its original condition and livery.

Imported from Malta, BUS 364, a wartime Bedford QL with a Leyland engine and a new Sammut body, is seen here in the UK while wearing the livery it carried on the Mediterranean island. (T. S. Blackman)

Built to 36-foot length, preserved ex-Walsall Corporation 56 (XDH 56G) is a Daimler Fleetline CRC6-36 that was new in December 1968 and carries Northern Counties dual door-bodywork. (Author's collection)

Starting life with Liverpool Corporation in September 1968 but restored in Merseyside PTE livery is MCW-bodied Leyland Panther PSUR1A/1R 1054 (FKF933G). (K. S. E. Till)

Numerically the last AEC Regent V to enter service in the UK, former Pontypridd UDC forward-entrance Willowbrook-bodied 8 (UTG 313G), which was new in March 1969, has been saved for posterity by the Cardiff Transport Preservation Group. (D. W. Rhodes)

New to Ulsterbus in May 1969, and serving all its operational life in Londonderry, dual-door Alexander-bodied Bristol RELL6L 1058 (905 8UZ) is seen here after undergoing a complete restoration. (Paul Savage)

Bristol's lightweight LH model is represented here by ECW-bodied VMO 234H, which was new to Thames Valley in November 1969, and happily still survives in preservation.

Typifying the ECW-bodied Bristol VRT, OCS 577H started life with Western SMT in November 1969, but was sold in 1973 for non-PSV use. It continued as such until 2012, when it was purchased for preservation. It is seen here after being restored in its original livery. (Neil Halliday)

Numerically the first AEC Swift purchased by London Transport, Marshall-bodied SM1 (AML 1H) entered service in January 1970, and is seen here preserved as a reminder of a once large, but unsuccessful, class of buses operated in the capital. (D. W. Rhodes)

New to Potteries Motor Traction in May 1970, 147 (BEH 147H) is an Alexander-bodied Daimler Fleetline SRG6LX-36, which is seen here immaculately restored to its original condition complete with NBC logos. (T. S. Blackman)

Entering service in January 1971, Park Royal-bodied DMS1 (EGP 1J), which is now preserved by the London Transport Museum, was the first of 2,646 Daimler Fleetlines to be purchased by London Transport, who deemed them to be unsuccessful despite the fact that many found new homes in the provinces, as well as overseas, where they enjoyed a normal lifespan. (Nigel Eadon-Clarke)

Although the Leyland Atlantean was regarded as a double-decker, a number were fitted with single-deck bodywork, as illustrated by former Portsmouth Corporation Seddon-bodied PDR2/1 190 (TBK 190K), which was new in August 1971. It is seen here at a preserved vehicle rally at Southsea in June 1998. (F. W. York)

Both having bodies built by their operator, Dublin-based CIE D415 (415 ZD) is a Leyland Atlantean PDR1A/1 that was new in September 1972, while alongside it is Leyland PD3/2 RA106 (HZA 231), which began life in September 1960 and features the typical CIE upper-deck front bulkhead window arrangement of the '50s and '60s. (Author's collection)

Typifying MCW's integrally built single-deck Metro Scania BR111MH is former Leicester City Transport dual-door 225 (ARY 225K), which began life in July 1972. (T. S. Blackman)

New in April 1972 to NBC-owned London Country Bus Services for use on Green Line operations, Park Royal-bodied AEC Reliance RP90 (JPA 190K) is seen after being restored to as new condition. (T. S. Blackman)

Rebuilt as shown here by Northern General in April 1972, now preserved 3000 (MCN 30K) started life in August 1958 as a normal MCCW-bodied Leyland PD3/4 with Tyneside Omnibus Co., registered NNL 49.

Built in June 1976 for operating on the Anglo-Scottish express coach services is forty-two-seat Alexander-bodied Seddon Pennine 7 MSF 750P, which was new to Eastern Scottish. (David Hudson collection)

New in September 1973 as a demonstrator for its manufacturer, unique flat-floor Leyland National RRM 148M was later sold to the West Midlands Police and then to Suffolk County Council before ultimately being purchased for preservation in 1992. Here, it is seen in fully restored condition. (T. S. Blackman)

Integrally constructed by Metro Cammell at Birmingham was the Scania-based Metropolitan, a 1976 example of which – former London Transport MD60 (KJD 260P) – is seen here in preservation with Ensign of Purfleet. (Nigel Eadon-Clarke)

Restored in Crosville's short-lived orange and green livery, Leyland National ENL930 (HFM 186N), which was new in February 1975, stands alongside Leyland National B-series SNL588 (JTU 588T), which entered service in February 1979 and is seen wearing Crosville's NBC green hue.

New in August 1977 as one of only nine Foden NC double-deckers ever built, now-preserved ex-West Midlands PTE Northern Counties-bodied 6300 (ROC 300R) is seen here in the midst of restoration in 2016. (Scott Poole)

Both Ailsa B55-10s with Alexander bodywork, ex-Eastern Scottish VV773 (CSG 773S), which was new in February 1978, and former London Buses V1 (A101 SUU), which began life in April 1984, are seen here at the Scottish Bus Museum after being purchased for preservation. (Author's collection)

The Bristol RELL6L chassis of XDU 396T was built in the UK in 1979 and then exported to New Zealand, where it was fitted with a dual-door Hess body for operation in Christchurch. After ending its working life with Bayline Coaches, it was purchased for preservation and returned to England in January 2011. It is seen here in the livery of its final owner. (Author's collection)

Although most Leyland Titan TN15s were purchased by London Transport, a few were bought by provincial operators, including 4002 (ANE 2T), which was new to SELNEC in April 1979. It is seen here after being preserved and restored to its original condition. (SELNEC Preservation Society)

Originally registered JKM 165V when new in August 1980, Duple-bodied Leyland Leopard PSU5C/4R MWV 840 has been restored in Hastings & District NBC-style livery. (T. S. Blackman)

Typical of the large number of Alexander-bodied Leyland Leopards purchased by the Scottish Bus Group, former Alexander Midland MPE374 (LMS 374W), which was new in August 1980, and has been superbly restored, is pictured here taking part in the 2013 HCVS Trans-Pennine Run.

New to Crosville in May 1981 as a conventional closed-top bus, ECW-bodied Bristol VRT YMB 512W was converted to open top in 1991. Seven years later it was subsumed into Arriva Wales, with whom it remained in service until its withdrawal and passage into preservation in 2011.

Typifying the Leyland National 2 is XUA 73X, which was new to West Riding in 1982, painted in NBC corporate red livery. It has since been restored in its operator's pre-National Bus Company colours, which it never wore in service. (David Hudson collection)

New to London Country in September 1982, fitted with an ECW coach body, Leyland Tiger WPH 139Y was given a new East Lancs body for Midland Red North in 1990. Seen here when preserved in 2009, it was unfortunately sold for scrap during the following year. (K. S. E. Till)

Representing the coach bodies built by ECW on Leyland Olympian chassis is former
Maidstone & District GKE 442Y, which began life in June 1983. It has been restored in the
NBC-style Invictaway livery that was used for operation on services from Kent to London.
(T. S. Blackman)

The Locomotors-bodied Quest B was a rare model, of which only six were built, all being purchased
by Merseyside PTE. Seen here after being purchased for preservation is C844 OBG, which was
new in October 1985 and was latterly operated by Millers, Foxton. (Author's collection)

Awaiting restoration in July 2017 are: ECW-bodied Leyland Olympian B516 UWW, which was new to West Yorkshire Road Car Co. in February 1985, but is seen here wearing Lincolnshire Road Car livery; ex-Huddersfield Corporation East Lancs-bodied AEC Regent III JVH 381; and former London Transport RT3458 (LYR 877).

Among the buses that started the minibus boom was Southern National's Ford Transit 300 (C862 DYD), which was new in August 1985. Fitted with a Dormobile body converted by Robin Hood (colloquially referred to as a 'bread van'), it is seen here after being preserved in its original livery. (Ian Winchester)

New to West Yorkshire PTE in July 1986 numbered 1807, C807 KBT is an Optare-bodied Leyland Cub CU435 and is seen here restored to its original livery.

Preserved by the London Transport Museum is Optare Citypacer-bodied Volkswagen LT55 minibus OY2 (C526 DYT), which was new to London Buses in July 1986 and was employed on its Roundabout network of services around Orpington.

New to Merseyside PTE in January 1987, 7685 (D685 SEM) is an Alexander-bodied Dodge S56 – a model that represents the size growth of minibuses. (K. S. E. Till)

Starting life with West Riding in March 1988, but preserved in Midland Red Coaches livery, is all-Leyland Royal Tiger RT E50 TYG. (D. W. Rhodes)

Superbly restored in West Midlands Travel Coventry livery is MCW Metrobus Mk II 3053 (F53 XOF), which was new in February 1989. (T. S. Blackman)

Starting life in November 1989 with West Yorkshire Road Car Co., integrally built Leyland Lynx 201 (G293 KWY) has been restored in Keighley & District livery, as seen here during its participation in an HVCS Trans-Pennine Run.

Leaving no doubt as to its pedigree, much-travelled Plaxton Paramount 3500-bodied Volvo B10M G21 CEH, which was new in January 1990, served with PMT, West Coast Motors and Eddie Brown before being acquired for preservation in 2015.

Representing the Wright-bodied step-entrance Dennis Dart, and painted in Gold Arrow livery, is DW15 (JDZ 2315), which was new to CentreWest in January 1991. It is now part of the London Transport Museum collection. (Nigel Eadon-Clarke)

Alexander-bodied tri-axle Leyland Olympian LM10 (FW 3858) from 1993 was first operated in Hong Kong by China Motor Bus and then New World First Bus before being repatriated in 2001 and re-registered K481 EUX to serve with First PMT, First Glasgow, and finally First Eastern Counties. It was then purchased for preservation in 2011 and returned to its original livery. (T. S. Blackman)

New in December 1993, and operated in London by First Capital, Mercedes-Benz 0530 Fuel Cell Bus ESQ64993 (LK53 MBV) has been preserved as an early example of alternative fuel propulsion, and is seen here at the London Transport Museum's Acton store in 2010.

One of a large number of Alexander PS-bodied Volvo B10Ms purchased by Stagecoach in the 1990s, 622 (L622 TDY) began life in June 1994 with Stagecoach Sussex Coastline and is seen here immaculately restored in its original livery. (Author's collection)

A trio of preserved former Black Prince, Morley, Optare-bodied Mercedes-Benz 0405s – N577 EUG, new in March 1996, TIL 7902 (ex-R202 YOR) dating from September 1997, and P441 SWX, new in December 1996 – surround ex-Halifax Joint Omnibus Committee Park Royal-bodied AEC Regent III 243 (AJX 369), which was new in December 1948 and is awaiting restoration.

Representing the once-familiar Alexander Royale-bodied Volvo Olympian is former Yorkshire Rider 30821 (R641 HYG), which was new in May 1998 numbered 5641, and is seen here in September 2016 wearing First's 'Barbie' livery.

Preserved by the London Bus Museum is S801 BWC, which was new in January 1999 and was the first Alexander-bodied Dennis Trident to be operated in the capital by Stagecoach London. (Nigel Eadon-Clarke)

Starting life with First Manchester in January 1999, but ending it with First West Yorkshire at Halifax in December 2015, is Wright-bodied Volvo B10BLE 60820 (S677 SVU), which is seen here preserved in its previous owner's current livery.

Among the first Optare Solos to be preserved is former West Midlands Travel 313 (T313 UOX), which was new in June 1999. (Author's collection)

Representing the new low-floor era within the preservation movement is Plaxton-bodied Dennis Dart SLF W404 UGM, which was new in June 2000 and is seen here in 2015 restored in Travel London livery.

Among the first bendibuses to be preserved in the UK is Mercedes-Benz 0530G BX02 YYZ, which began life with London General in May 2002 and latterly served with Go Ahead subsidiary Wilts & Dorset, painted in Bournemouth University livery. (D. W. Rhodes)